The Purim Story Told By Esther

**We're working on an app! Join us now
& get it for free when we launch.**

Unlimited illustrated children's stories like this one that
teach **your** values (history, religion, family, courage,
kindness, and much more) in one app including
animations, music, read aloud, and even an option to
insert familiar family faces into the story!

Have you heard the story of Purim? You haven't?! Well, fortunately, I was there! So let me tell you everything that happened.

To start, we have to travel back more than 1,000 years to the old country of Persia. My story takes place so long ago that the country isn't even called Persia anymore, we call it Iran!

My name is Esther, and I grew up in Persia with my amazing cousin, Mordecai.
We were like best friends!
Wherever I went, Mordecai was always close behind.

One day, Mordecai came rushing through the front
door, with sweat dripping down his face.
"Have... have... have you heard?!" he panted.
"Queen Vashti, she has been banished!"

"Banished?!" I gasped.
"What do you mean banished?!
Who could banish the Queen?"

Mordecai explained,
"The King, of course. I heard
rumours that she disobeyed him,
so he kicked her out of Persia
never to return."

"But we can't have a king without a queen!" I complained.

Fortunately, the King already had a plan for that. With Queen Vashti gone, he had a spare seat to fill in his throne room and he wanted to find the most beautiful woman in all of Persia. So the King ran the biggest beauty contest the country had ever seen!

"You have to enter, Eshter!" my friends insisted.
"Oh, I don't know about that," I blushed.
"I don't think the King would ever choose me..."

But I was wrong! One week later, I was crowned the most beautiful woman in the country and the new Queen of Persia. There was just one problem. No one realised I was Jewish, and I wasn't about to tell them!

"All hail, Queen Esther!"

"Hip hip, hooray.
Hip hip, hooray.
Hip hip, hooray."

Becoming Queen was so new and exciting, but I missed parts of my old life. A weird man by the name of Haman was always hanging around the palace to talk to the King. After a while, he was promoted to become the King's most powerful advisor, but I had a strange feeling about him.

I wished I could talk to my friends about Haman, but I couldn't see them as often as I wanted, and I no longer had Mordecai by my side every single day. But, when he visited the palace, it was always the highlight of my day.

Until one day, Mordecai arrived with some rather worrying news...
"I... I... I... heard a rumour," he panted.
I couldn't help but laugh, "Why are you always out of breath, cousin?"

"I ran straight here as soon as I heard," Mordecai revealed. "There is a plot to kill the king!"

"Oh my!" I screamed.

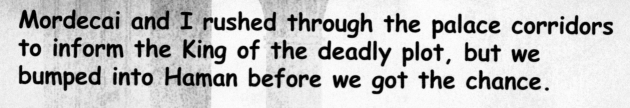

Mordecai and I rushed through the palace corridors to inform the King of the deadly plot, but we bumped into Haman before we got the chance.

"Who do we have here?" Haman sneered.
"This is my cousin, Mordecai," I answered.
"Mordecai, this is Haman, the King's chief advisor."

"Aren't you going to bow to me, boy?" Haman grunted. "How dare you not bow!"

"I only bow to my King and my Queen," Mordecai insisted.

From that day on, Haman held a grudge against Mordecai and the rest of the Jewish people. He wanted to destroy every single Jewish person living in Persia, just because he didn't like them. I wanted to visit the King and tell him what an awful person his chief advisor was, but I was scared. I didn't want to be banished from Persia like Queen Vashti! Then who would save the Jewish people?!

So Mordecai and I came up with a plan...

I invited the King to a banquet in the palace, where he could meet Mordecai and hear all about the deadly plot. The King was so impressed by Mordecai's loyalty that he honoured him at the banquet with a special gold medal. Mordecai was definitely in the King's good books!

But there was no time for celebration because I had a speech to give.

I cleared my throat and stood up in front of the King and all the Persian people. It was time for everyone to know what a horrible person Haman really was.

"My King," I began. "I am so happy that we put an end to the plot against your life. But I'm afraid I have discovered another plot to kill me, your Queen."

"What?!" the King gasped. "Whoever would do such a thing."
"The man responsible is sitting right in this room," I revealed. "HAMAN!"

The palace fell into silence and Haman looked more shocked than anyone.
"I... I... I... b-b-but... what on Earth do you mean?" he stammered nervously.

"My King, Haman has put out an order to kill every single Jewish person living in Persia and that includes your Queen. For I am Jewish. So, if you agree with Haman's horrible plot, then you also agree that I should die along with my people. Don't you see that this is wrong? You need to put an end to this plot!" I cried.

The King looked at me, then he looked across at Haman, then back at me again.
"ENOUGH!" he bellowed. "I have made my decision! No Jews are to be killed in Persia while I am King. Now take this man away!"
The guards escorted Haman to the palace prison and the people of Persia celebrated.

"Hip hip, hooray.
Hip hip, hooray.
Hip hip, hooray."

Haman was gone. The Jews were saved. And Mordecai even earned an important promotion!

And that is the tale of Purim!

Remember, kids... always stand up for what you believe in! Sometimes, when things need to change, it is up to us to change them!